IMAGES
of America

POTSDAM

A VIEW OF POTSDAM C. 1935. This photograph shows the Maple Street entrance to the village, with Potsdam's two bridges spanning the Racquette River. To the left, between the bridges, is Fall Island, site of a number of businesses. Trinity Church, on the island, is to the right.

IMAGES
of America
POTSDAM

Potsdam Public Museum

ARCADIA
PUBLISHING

Copyright © 2004 by Potsdam Public Museum
ISBN 978-1-5316-2142-1

Published by Arcadia Publishing
Charleston, South Carolina

Library of Congress Catalog Card Number: 2004107286

For all general information contact Arcadia Publishing at:
Telephone 843-853-2070
Fax 843-853-0044
E-mail sales@arcadiapublishing.com
For customer service and orders:
Toll-Free 1-888-313-2665

Visit us on the Internet at www.arcadiapublishing.com

THE CIVIC CENTER ON PARK STREET, 1935. This view of the civic center complex shows, from left to right, the village auditorium, the municipal offices, and the Potsdam Public Library. The complex was built of rough-ashlar sandstone from Potsdam quarries. In 1933, the Universalist church building, erected in 1876 (at right end of complex in photograph), was given to the village to be used as a library. The church building was remodeled, the tower was removed, and the entrance was relocated to the Park Street side. In 1934, the opera house was torn down, and the stone therefrom was used in the construction of the civic center. In 1940, the Potsdam Public Museum was established to house a collection of English china given by Mr. and Mrs. F. P. Burnap. The museum was housed in the basement of the library building. In 1976, the library moved to the former village auditorium (at far left here). Since 1977, the museum has occupied the entire former Universalist church building.

Contents

Acknowledgments		6
Introduction		7
1.	Industry, Mercantile, and Farming	9
2.	Education and Culture	31
3.	Worship	47
4.	People and Homes	55
5.	Everyday Life	77
6.	Potsdam, the Nation, and the World	101
7.	Special Days	109

Acknowledgments

The photographs and information presented in this book are from the archives of the Potsdam Public Museum. We are very grateful to all the people who have added to our photograph collection and archival material over the years. Thank you to the Friends of the Potsdam Museum for their financial assistance with this project. Our special thanks to Professor Arthur L. Johnson, a member of our museum board of trustees and the board of the Friends of the Potsdam Museum, for his support and willingness to contribute an introduction to our book.

We trust that not only will our book tell much of the story of Potsdam, New York, but that it will also indicate the extent of the research materials which the Potsdam Museum makes available to the public.

—The Potsdam Public Museum
Director: Betsy L. Travis
Staff: Joanne Swift, Susan Thacher, Peter Wallen, Pamela Whalen

INTRODUCTION

Potsdam is at once typical of a northeastern college town and unique in its history and character. We who live in it and love it walk or drive the village's streets as if they have always been there, as if Potsdam has always been as it is and somehow always will be. Why should we care what happened here a century or two ago? And yet care we must, because the past is part of who we are as a community and as individuals. We are, in part, who we were.

Think of the ethnic groups that have composed this community, beginning with the English Americans from New York and New England. Speculators like the Clarksons from New York City saw commercial possibilities here at the falls of the Racquette River. Farmers came from New England when the population of that region had exhausted the good farmlands. These Yankees brought with them their passion for religion and for education. They founded Protestant congregations, first Presbyterian and then Episcopal. They founded a school as well: St. Lawrence Academy. Not many years later, the Irish immigrants and French Canadians came to work the mills, lumber camps, and the railroad, which reached Potsdam in 1856. The Irish and the French brought their fervent Roman Catholicism, and this led to the founding of St. Mary's Parish. Later in the century, Jewish merchants from New York came, built stores, brought their families, and formed a community and synagogue, Temple Beth-El. Other ethnic groups contributed, coming to work in the local industries, including the red sandstone quarry upriver, a creamery, and wood industries—the remnants of which are today Potsdam Hardwoods and the paper mill north of the village.

In the 20th century, education became Potsdam's major business. St. Lawrence Academy, founded by Yankee pioneers in 1816, was the acorn from which grew the Potsdam Normal School, which later became the Teachers College and still later a liberal arts college, SUNY Potsdam. Its sister institution, Clarkson University, was started as the Thomas S. Clarkson Memorial School of Technology by the Clarkson family. A large percentage of Potsdam people work for one or the other of these centers of higher learning.

Potsdam grew in the 19th century, and businessmen erected the buildings that still stand on Market Street with their elaborate Victorian facades. Hotels catered to salesmen and other travelers. In the 20th century, the automobile changed everything. Earlier modes of transportation, like the horse and buggy, gradually disappeared. Even passenger trains, once so important to Potsdam, no longer connected the area to major cities to the north and south. The railroad station, which stood empty for a long time, eventually became a restaurant. Retail businesses could be found not only in the village center, but also in shopping centers a mile north on Market Street.

While fires have destroyed some of the village's older buildings, the stone churches have endured. The handsome stone Universalist church has become the Potsdam Public Museum, a stained-glass window attesting to its former status. The village offices remain, accessible through a new building that houses the police and rescue squad. Next to the offices, what was once the civic center auditorium is now the attractive village library.

The Racquette River has come to be recognized as an asset, and efforts have been made to beautify Ives Park and Lions Park (Fall Island), and to provide picnic areas below the dams. The river, which was a highway for logs in the lumbering days, now provides recreational opportunities for canoes and kayaks from May to September. The dams erected by Niagara Mohawk Power Company in the 1920s and 1930s have made the river wider and shallower in the village, but the waterway nevertheless remains an attractive feature.

This photographic history will portray many of the changes Potsdam has undergone. Since the mid-1800s, photography has made history more vivid. With photographs, we can look through the eyes of our predecessors and see the world as they saw it, albeit in black and white. We can know the past in our hearts as well as in our minds. Even those who would not trouble to read a dense and detailed history of Potsdam will perhaps leaf through this book and come away with some solid impressions of at least two-thirds of the 200 years of Potsdam's existence.

—Arthur L. Johnson
2004

One
Industry, Mercantile, and Farming

The Leete Foundry and Machine Shop, c. 1920. Located on Maple Street (Fall Island), this business dealt in the manufacture and repair of water wheels, machinery that was used by lumber mills, box factories, and quarries. Stock consisted of hardware, stoves, and agricultural implements. In 1920, owner Charles Leete employed 12 men at this shop.

THE RACQUETTE RIVER PAPER COMPANY, C. 1924. In 1892, George Wing Sisson Sr. bought the site of the old Union Mill at Unionville, on the east side of the Racquette River, for $50,000. The old sawmill was torn down and the Racquette River Paper Company was built. A new wooden dam and flume were also constructed. Production began with three wood pulp grinders and one paper machine. In the early days, the mill produced only a few grades of paper, including "Manilla, Butcher Fibre, and general Wrappers." Eventually, the Racquette River Paper Company became known for specialty papers such as filter, map, and Braille papers, and embossed and printed papers for national companies including Sears, Montgomery Ward, and Rexall. The entire plant was rebuilt between 1908 and 1910, making it among the most modern paper mills in the country. By 1951, four generations of Sissons were involved in the company. One of the few 19th-century industries to have survived in Potsdam, the Racquette River Paper Company is known today as the Mead Specialty Paper Company.

LOGGERS OF THE RACQUETTE RIVER PAPER COMPANY, C. 1907. Located three miles north of Potsdam, the mill produced ground wood, chemical pulp, and later, specialty papers. It was one of the largest employers in Potsdam for many years.

STONE CUTTERS, C. 1900. Workers line up for a photograph outside the Clarkson Sandstone Cutting shop on Pine Street. Stone for home and business foundations, walls, sidewalks, and architectural elements was cut here. The cutters are representative of the various immigrant groups that came to America, including the French, Irish, and Italian. The shop was in operation from 1877 to 1921.

KNITTING MILL WORKERS, C. 1898. Employees of the Potsdam Knitting Company assemble in front of the company's Mill No. 1, located on Fall Island. The business offered "dyeing, washing, finishing, knitting, and drying." Constructed in 1892 as the Potsdam Sugar of Milk factory, the structure was one of many that burned down in 1900. At the time of the fire, the building was being rented by Dr. Hervey D. Thatcher for his baking powder and paper pail business.

SWEETSER (SIC) & SON EMPLOYEES, MAY 4, 1925. The ladies' lingerie business Thomas M. Greig opened in 1901 developed into the Greig Muslin Underwear Co. The factory was located at 5–7 Maple Street, in the Manley Block on Fall Island. Some years later, G. E. and J. Sweetzer opened their men's shirt manufacturing business at the same location. The company was financed by 20 Potsdam businessmen, and was managed by Julian P. Heath and Frank L. Perkins (standing, third and fourth from left). The business closed near the end of 1928.

RILEY & O'BRIEN MARBLE WORKS, FALL ISLAND, C. 1868. Riley & O'Brien Marble Works, also called Bayside Marble Works and Potsdam Marble Works, was established about 1850. The business was located at 6 and 8 Maple Street. They specialized in "Monuments, Head-stones, Tablets, Mantels & Table Tops. American & Italian Marble. Satisfaction Guaranteed."

BATCHELDER & SONS FURNITURE (RUINS), C. 1915. Owned and operated for over 85 years by the Batchelder family, this furniture factory on Fall Island was founded in 1841 as Batchelder & Badlam. The company offered a variety of products, including pianos, furniture, and cabinetry, as well as undertaking services. Batchelder's had a salesroom located on Market Street and later on Raymond Street. This factory survived at least five fires, and twice escaped being swept from the island by flood.

GO AHEAD AND EAT IT! 1923. The advertising on John P. McGraw's "rolling cash" delivery truck, pictured here in 1923, urged the public to consider ice cream as "food." The business was located at 22 Depot Street.

GEORGE BULLES JR. AND "HIRED MAN," C. 1933. George Bulles Jr. (right) and son Berton stand beside his truck in front of the Pert House on Elm Street. George Jr. drove a hack for his father before buying his first truck in 1919, a secondhand Model T, which he used to carry mail between the post office and the depot. Julia Crane was a regular customer for piano moving, because instruments that George transported never needed tuning.

DELAVAL DAIRY EQUIPMENT, C. 1915. This display at the Potsdam Fairgrounds exhibited technology that changed the dairy industry. Before the 1870s, the "Cooley System" required the use of large quantities of water, ice, and hard labor to produce butter. The cream separator invented by Carl de Laval (1845–1913) powered by a hand crank and later a motor, used centrifugal force to accomplish in minutes what had previously taken hours.

THE GRIST MILL, MAPLE STREET, C. 1950. This sandstone grist mill, built in 1835, had replaced an earlier mill. The business continued in operation until about 1914. Later used as a warehouse, the building was razed in 1972 to make way for a donut shop.

AT THE SIGN OF THE GOLDEN HORSESHOE, C. 1882. Tailors for Heath, Landers, and Company pose bravely on the ledge outside the second-floor windows, above the retail establishment at 26 Market Street. Clothing establishments occupied this site, located next to the Sewall Raymond Building, for approximately 70 years.

THE SHOPS AT 18–20 MAIN STREET, THE 1890S. Talented inventor Edmond Martin ran a busy tin shop. Martin had at least four inventions to his credit between 1890 and 1904. Thomas P. Woods's Bakery, established in 1891, was next door. Thomas Woods was in business for 52 years at various locations in town. The *St. Lawrence Herald*, upstairs, was published by Rollin C. Sumner.

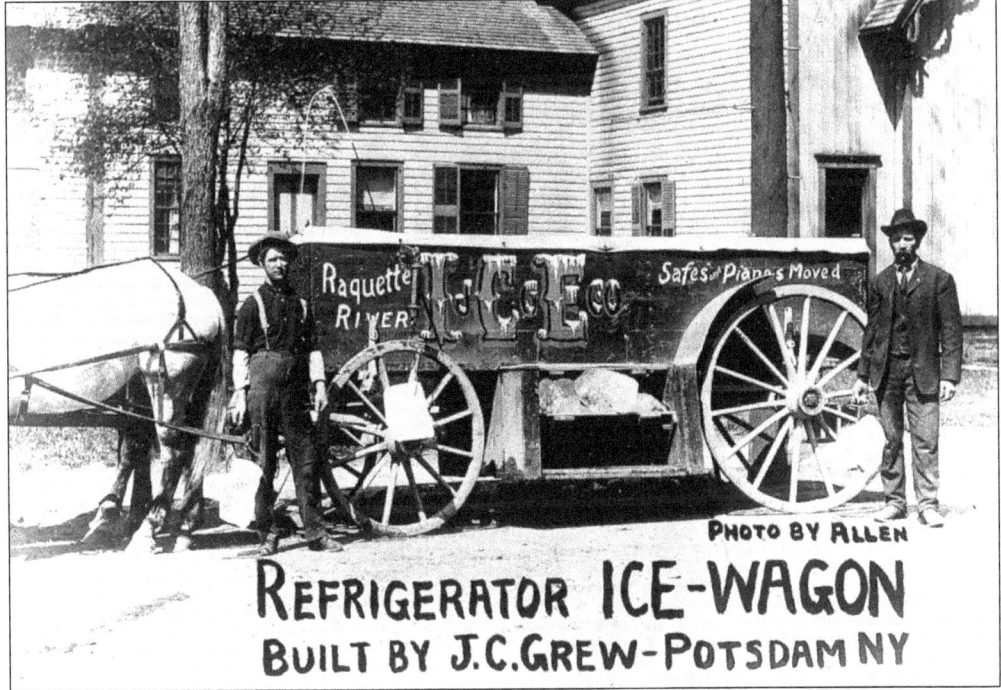

RAQUETTE RIVER ICE, 1908. William Sullivan, blacksmith (left), and Joseph Grew, contractor, stand with tongs at the ready, at the corner of Depot and Market Streets. Sullivan gave "special attention" to "lame and interfering horses" at his shop behind Lenney's grocers on Main Street. Grew was known for having done the excavation for Clarkson's Old Main building (1895).

JOE BROWN'S BLACKSMITH SHOP, C. 1913. Blacksmith James D. Jannette (left) and retired farmer John W. Parker (center) stand with Joseph P. Brown at his 15 1/2 Main Street shop. By 1924, the shop had become a garage.

A BOTTLE-TOP STAMP MACHINE, C. 1888. Fred Hayes, employee of the Thatcher Manufacturing Company, uses a foot-powered press to punch out milk bottle caps from a strip of cardboard treated with wax. Either Hervey Thatcher or his brothers-in-law, Samuel and Harvey Barnhart, invented this paper cap for sealing glass milk bottles; the Barnharts' names appear on the 1889 patent. The stamp machine was soon replaced by a power-driven (probably steam) press.

THOMAS WOODS GROCERIES, C. 1910. In 1897, Thomas Woods (standing, third from right) established his first grocery business. This store at 13 Main Street was a fixture in the community into the 1940s. An avid sportsman, Woods was a primary source of supplies for many local hunting camps.

THE ALBION HOTEL, ELM STREET, C. 1915. The earliest section of the Albion Hotel was built by Martin V. B. Ives and Hallen Ives in 1868 and was called the European House. In 1874, the Ives brothers sold the hotel to C. R. Holmes, who enlarged it and renamed it the Albion. During its many years of service to the area, the Albion was a favorite with traveling men, sportsmen venturing into the Adirondacks, and locals enjoying a good meal and socialization. In order to best transport customers to and from the train station and other destinations, the hotel had several "buses," in addition to Mr. Bulles's hack service. The Albion survived several fires and had various owners. The building was razed in 1973.

T. H. Perrin and Company, Druggists, c. 1919. The building at 19 Market Street housed drug stores from the 1860s to the 1990s. Originally built by Dr. Hervey D. Thatcher, over the years the location was the home of the Brown and Perrin, T. H. Perrin, and B. O. Kinney stores.

The Albion Hotel Bar, Elm Street, the 1920s. The bartender is Fred Cassner.

EDWARD JOY'S HARNESS SHOP, C. 1900. Located at 9 Main Street, Edward Joy's Harness Shop opened in May 1876, and was in operation for over 45 years. He was a leading dealer and manufacturer of harnesses, saddles, and horse furnishings. Edward Joy is on the right. Notice the sandstone sidewalk in the foreground.

THE DUFFY-RIVERS COMPANY, C. 1911. Elaborately decorated in the Stars and Stripes, a Glidden Tour–winning motor car announces the fall opening of the Duffy-Rivers Company. Located at 5–7 Market Street, the business sold dry goods, cloaks, suits, and millinery. The store's annual fall sale coincided with the Potsdam Fair, which featured a parade of decorated automobiles.

MCCARTHY'S, C. 1935. The Duffy-Rivers Company at 5–7 Market Street was succeeded in the mid-1930s by a clothing store run by Jerry McCarthy. This Romanesque-style building was constructed in 1888 by Charles Cox, using the rough-ashlar method of laying sandstone. In 1948, Lewis and Company, women's clothiers, moved from 9 Market Street to this location.

POTSDAM ELECTRIC LIGHT & POWER COMPANY SERVICE TRUCK NO. 1, C. 1913. In 1913, this Model T Ford Service Truck was one of three vehicles operating out of Potsdam for the Hannawa Falls Electric Light and Power Co. Arthur Cassada, a Clarkson graduate and electrician, was the truck's first driver. The vehicle's service to the company was short. During the severe ice storm of 1913, the truck's top was torn off when it struck a guy wire.

THE PEOPLES BANK, 1910. Erected in 1853 for the Frontier Bank (1853–1866), Potsdam's first banking institution also housed the National Bank of Potsdam (1866–1897) and the Peoples Bank (1897–1924), shown here. Since then, a series of businesses have occupied the building, which is still in place today.

THE POTSDAM FRUIT MARKET, C. 1910. Louis Lagona stands in the doorway of his store at 3 Elm Street, next to the Albion Hotel. For sale are watermelons, pineapples, bananas, and other fruits. Inside you could purchase ice cream made with milk from Meadow Brook Farm.

THE WHEEL CAFÉ, C. 1915. Benjamin D. Miles invites you to stop by his elaborately painted lunch car and "Eat a Bite." The café was located on the corner of Water Street, next to Tom Nadeau's barbershop.

TIME FOR LUNCH, C. 1915. Floyd Senter and Benjamin Miles served sandwiches, pie, and coffee at the Wheel Café. By 1919, the lunch wagon was owned by William Jardine.

HERBERT W. FEARL, C. 1915. Among the most progressive merchants in Potsdam, Fearl began his career working in real estate. Subsequently, from about 1892 to 1912, he was superintendent of Clarkson Manufacturing Co. And by 1907, he owned farmers' sheds and sold wood, oil, and gasoline. Fearl owned property that began at 12 Depot Street, ran through to Raymond Street, and extended to the railroad. In 1915, when this photograph was taken, Fearl employed seven men and owned barns, a blacksmith shop, tenements, and a fruit store.

THE AMERICAN GASOLINE STATION, 1923. Herbert Fearl ran this garage on Depot Street through the early 1930s. He also repaired all kinds of machinery and sold farm implements. The poster to the left announces a J. Sullivan Holstein auction on August 22, 1923.

THE L. PINCUS CLOTHING STORE, C. 1925. The "one-price store that saves you money" sold menswear at 14 Market Street from 1919 through 1944. Louis Pincus resided in New York City. His sons Harry and Nathan roomed at the Albion Hotel on Elm Street.

THE FREDERICK R. HAYWOOD JEWELRY STORE, C. 1930. The jewelry store at 18 Market Street was opened by Charles E. Haywood in the early 1900s, with his son Frederick serving as watchmaker. Frederick took over the business in the 1920s, and it remained at this location for over 30 years.

ICE HARVESTING, C. 1880. Before the invention of modern refrigeration, ice was stored in warehouses along the Racquette River for use through the year. This crew from Cornell & Son watched for weather conditions to be just right, toward the end of January, when the ice would snap and crack with a loud boom. Then, working night and day, the crew marked and cut the ice into grids, sawing and barring off sections. Blocks of ice were then "canalled" to the icehouse on Water Street, where they would be stored in sawdust.

GEORGE MATHEWS'S AUTO DISPLAY, AT THE POTSDAM FAIR, C. 1917. George Mathews, whose father began selling Fords in Potsdam around 1910, sold Dodge Brothers motor cars from his Club Garage on Elm Street, opposite the Albion House. Here, Mathews displays several models next to Floral Hall at the Potsdam Fair.

THE NEW WINDSOR HOTEL, C. 1913. Located at 11 Market Street, the New Windsor Hotel, W. L. Redmond proprietor, occupied a building constructed in the 1860s in the Italianate style. The hotel was situated between the Cash Hardware Company and Smith and Smith Hardware. Previously the site of a woolen factory in the 1830s, 11 Market Street would become the home of Endicott-Johnson Shoes in the 1930s.

THE A & P TEA COMPANY, 1924. The "Golden Rule Dinner" sign in the window of the A & P, 12 Main Street, promoted an "International Golden Rule Sunday" to be observed in 14 countries on December 7, 1924. Customers were encouraged to "Dine for one day on the foods which are served to Orphans in the care of the NEAR EAST RELIEF." Suggested foods for the observance were rice, beans, canned milk, and macaroni.

A HOLSTEIN COW. Cows and dairying have been a part of the North Country economy since the settlement of the area. The development of the refrigerated railroad car widened the distribution of milk and milk products. Introduced into northern New York in the 1870s, the Holstein has been a favorite with local farmers over the years because of its high milk production and hardiness to cold climates.

TRANSPORTING CHICKENS, C. 1920. Workers transport Benson's Leghorns in wooden cages aboard a wagon. Fred C. Benson was the proprietor of Central Meat and Grocery Market at 33 Market Street. Potsdam's depot is to the right of the wagon.

COURIER AND FREEMAN, THE 1920S. The first newspaper in town was the *Potsdam Gazette*, established by Frederick Powell and Zenas Clark in 1816. It survived about seven years and was succeeded by a number of other local publications. The *Courier-Freeman*, established about 1861, was the result of the consolidation of the *Courier and Journal* and the *Northern Freeman*. Fay, Baker, and Co. were the proprietors. The *Courier-Freeman* office was located on the corner of Market and Depot Streets until 1964, when the staff moved to new offices. This newspaper continued publication until 1989, when it merged with the *Massena-Observer* to become the *Courier-Observer*. Standing at the entrance to the *Courier-Freeman* office are, from left to right, Frank Cubley, Henry Buchman, Louis Baker, Henry Juen, and Dave Weller.

Two

EDUCATION AND CULTURE

ST. LAWRENCE ACADEMY BUILDINGS AND THE PRESBYTERIAN CHURCH, C. 1854. The St. Lawrence Academy grew out of the first schoolhouse/church built by Benjamin Raymond. The academy was located on Park Street, across from the present civic center. The North Academy Building (left) was built in 1825. The South Academy Building (far right), erected in 1835, housed the Teacher Training Program of the Rev. Asa Brainerd, principal. The Presbyterian brick church (center) was constructed in 1854.

St. Lawrence Academy's North Building, c. 1865. The North Academy Building, erected in 1825, was located on Elm Street, nearly opposite the present-day Presbyterian church. The building was constructed of Potsdam sandstone using the slab and binder masonry technique. The cupola held the bell from the original St. Lawrence Academy, the one-story frame building that was used as both school and church. In 1816, the New York State Board of Regents officially chartered the academy. At that time, the school had 42 students; by 1825, the number of students had increased to 247. Potsdam-area boys and girls between the ages of 10 and 20 attended the academy, as well as residents of Clinton and Oneida counties and Canada. Students paid a quarterly tuition fee. In 1867, Potsdam became one of four normal school sites in New York state. As part of the arrangement, all St. Lawrence Academy properties were deeded to New York state for the new Normal and Training School. In 1868, the buildings were torn down and the Potsdam Normal School was constructed at the site.

POTSDAM NORMAL SCHOOL, C. 1880. The first Potsdam Normal School was built in 1868, between Elm and Main Streets on the site of the former St. Lawrence Academy. This building was torn down and rebuilt in 1917.

STONE WORKERS AT STOWELL ANNEX, MAIN STREET, 1888–1889. In 1888, work began on a three-story sandstone annex that would be connected by a corridor to the original Potsdam Normal School building. The annex was named for Dr. Thomas Stowell, an innovative early administrator at the normal school. Part of the new annex contained a gymnasium. Stowell promoted the importance of organized physical activities, and during his tenure the school began sponsoring sports teams.

THE POTSDAM NORMAL BASEBALL TEAM, C. 1893. The members of the squad and their hometowns are, from left to right, as follows: (first row) Dr. Deans, Potsdam; Web Snell, Theresa; and Frank Buck, Gouverneur; (second row) Jack Wright and Charles Putnam, Alexandria Bay; Dr. D. F. Burke, Potsdam; Dr. Roy Porter, Malone; and Frank Wires, Potsdam; (third row) Ed Kirby, manager, Syracuse; Sanco George, Theresa; John Hosmer, Potsdam; and Charles Vert, Plattsburgh.

A NORMAL SCHOOL PERFORMANCE, C. 1888. Francis Ten Eyck Sisson, tenor, is shown here (on the right) in a normal school production. Sisson, the son of George Wing Sisson Sr., president of the Potsdam Paper Company, studied voice in Potsdam and in Manhattan. He taught at the Burlington School of Music, directed the Potsdam Choral Society, and appeared often in comic opera throughout northern New York.

THE CRANE NORMAL INSTITUTE OF MUSIC, c. 1905. Julia E. Crane, director of the Crane Normal Institute of Music, purchased this house at 60 Main Street in 1896. The house, located next door to the normal school, served as Crane's residence and as a home for the institute. The house offered space for vocal instruction and practice. By 1910, more room was needed and was provided in the normal school building.

LAYING THE CORNERSTONE OF THE NEW NORMAL SCHOOL BUILDING, AUGUST 15, 1917. The officers and chaplain of Racquette River Masonic Lodge No. 213 conduct the ceremony; the placing of the stone is in the hands of the project's superintendent Carl E. Arenander and stonecutter S. Locaseio. The cornerstones of the St. Lawrence Academy and the old normal school were re-laid, with the new stone at the northeast corner of the building.

THE POTSDAM NORMAL SCHOOL'S INDOOR BASEBALL TEAM, 1905. Potsdam's first game of the season was held on February 8, 1905, when Potsdam defeated Clarkson Tech 45-36 in the normal school gym. According to the February 10 issue of the *Herald-Recorder*, Flora Orr (seated, center) recorded two triple plays. Because the baseball team competed with the basketball team for use of the gym, the paper recorded, "It is not surprising that some of them became rather bewildered and threw the ball in the wrong place at different stages of the game." Members of the baseball squad are (listed by numbers written on photograph) 1. Alice Sanford, 2. Grace Maine, 3. Flora Orr, 4. Millie Botsford, 5. Theodora Mayham, 6. Grace Drury, 7. Martha Clark, 8. Ellen Canton, 9. Edna Robertson, and 10. Anna Schuyler.

THE SENIOR CHORUS, 1926. The Potsdam Normal School chorus and orchestra is directed by Prof. Franklin H. Bishop. The organist is Miss H. M. Hewitt, and the pianist is Miss ? Jones.

HMS PINAFORE, 1927. Students present Gilbert & Sullivan's HMS *Pinafore* at Potsdam Normal School on February 24, 1927. Franklin H. Bishop directs the orchestra.

THE THOMAS S. CLARKSON MEMORIAL COLLEGE OF TECHNOLOGY, C. 1896. "Old Main," as it is now called, is located on Main Street, and is the original site of today's Clarkson University. The building is constructed of Potsdam red sandstone from the Clarkson quarries, cut in the rough-ashlar method. After the tragic death of their brother Thomas in a quarry accident in 1894, Elizabeth, Frederica, and Lavinia Clarkson wished to honor him both as a leading citizen of Potsdam and as an advocate of educational opportunities. In keeping with his ideals, they established the Thomas S. Clarkson Memorial College of Technology to teach technical skills and engineering. The college opened its doors to students in 1896. The first class of students was composed of eight men and four women. Women were accepted into the college's domestic engineering program until 1907, when Clarkson College became a male-only institution. It remained such until 1964, when one woman gained admission, and thereafter women were again accepted. Beginning in 1956, Clarkson College started to expand to the Clarkson Estate, or Clarkson Hill, located on outer Maple Street. Today, most of Clarkson's facilities are located there. In 1984, the college gained university status from the New York State Board of Regents and is now Clarkson University.

THE CLARKSON FRESHMAN BASEBALL TEAM, CLASS OF 1911. The team is ready to play ball.

CLARKSON'S MACHINE SHOP, 1930. Instructor Archie Ephraim Sutherland observes the work of Richard Van Camp, class of 1931 (at center of photograph). Sutherland Hall, where this shop was located, was built in 1919 and named after the instructor. Archie Sutherland grew up in the Potsdam area, and taught students to weld with a forge, anvil, and hammer. Referred to as "Old Archie," Sutherland was on the faculty for 35 years, retiring in 1937.

CLARKSON MEN WELCOMING ALUMNI, 1949. Brothers at Lambda Iota fraternity, 30 Elm Street, welcome alumni and celebrate their 30th year together. This house was purchased in 1922. In 1960, the group joined the national fraternity Delta Upsilon, changing their name but keeping "the big white house on Elm Street."

THE POTSDAM RACING TEAM, 1894. From left to right are the following: (sitting) William McCormick and F. Dempsy; (kneeling) B. Everett, W. W. G. Peck, and H. H. Swift; (standing) G. P. Benson, Meryl Crammer, William Wallen, unidentified, and William O'Brien.

THE POTSDAM VILLAGE BASEBALL TEAM, C. 1890. Members of the squad are, from left to right, as follows: (first row) Bert Snell, Mike Gallagher, and Greg Rundell; (second row) John Mullen, Jim Doyle, Harvey Story (manager), and Dick Nolan; (third row) Frank Hires, Gilbert French, and Silas Stone.

THE RACQUETTE RIVER PAPER COMPANY BASEBALL TEAM, C. 1920. This team was sponsored by the Racquette River Paper Company.

THE KNIGHTS OF THE MACCABEES BASEBALL TEAM, C. 1910. This baseball team was sponsored by the Knights of the Maccabees, a fraternal order of Potsdam businessmen.

THE BLUE RAMBLERS HOCKEY TEAM, 1930. Team members are, from left to right, as follows: (first row) Lynn Robinson, Harold Smith, and Willard Robinson; (second row) ? Kane, Howard Smith (manager), John La Parco, Alvin Earle, Paul Perry, and Donald Swan.

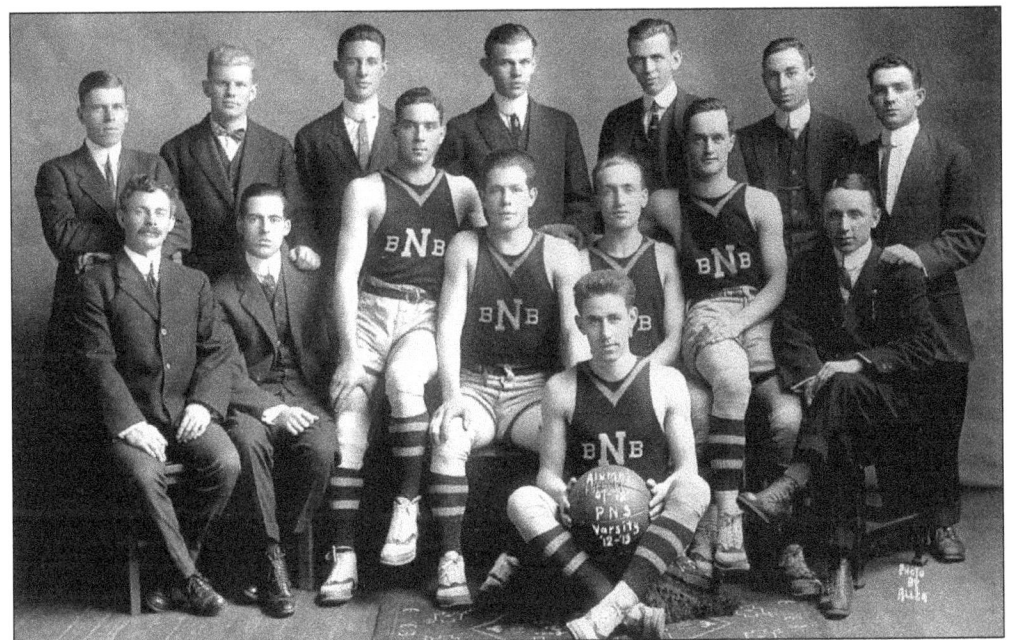

PROFESSOR BLOOD AND THE 1912–1913 NORMAL SCHOOL BASKETBALL TEAM. Prof. Ernest Blood (front row, far left) poses with his high school team that defeated City College of New York 34-8. When asked for a rematch in New York City, Potsdam obliged and won 26-21. Over the years, Blood's teams had a record of 72 wins and 2 losses.

THE POTSDAM NORMAL HIGH SCHOOL FOOTBALL TEAM, 1921. Sporting new uniforms, the Potsdam Normal School's football squad sits for a team photograph with their coach, J. R. Maxcy. Described as "light but fast," the team played a five-game schedule in which they defeated Ogdensburg, Canton, Malone, and Massena, and tied Gouverneur. In a rematch with Massena for the Northern New York League championship, Potsdam was defeated before a crowd of 3,000 at Weekes Athletic Field in Canton.

DISTRICT SCHOOL NO. 30, PINE STREET, 1924. The Pine Street School was one of three district schools in Potsdam in the late 19th century. Classes were held there even after Lawrence Avenue Elementary School opened in 1958. In 1969, at the request of the village board, the fire department destroyed the Pine Street School. The land eventually became part of a recreation park.

POTSDAM HIGH SCHOOL, C. 1945. In 1917, a contract was made between the village of Potsdam and the New York State Education Department to house the community's high school students in a wing of the State Normal School. This contract would expire in 1933, but by 1928, due to overcrowding, the citizens of Potsdam already were taking steps to build a new, separate high school. The Potsdam Fairgrounds on Leroy Street was the chosen site.

SECOND GRADE, 1921–1922. These smiling second-graders attended Potsdam Normal School's practice school.

BIKE RIDERS, C. 1950. Children from the Congdon Campus School line up with their bicycles. In 1931 the practice school building was dedicated to Randolph T. Congdon, principal of the Potsdam Normal School.

THE DISTRICT SCHOOL NO. 17, THE CORNER OF MARKET AND ELDERKIN STREETS, C. 1888. Teacher Betsy Sanford Sherburne leads her students through an arithmetic lesson in a classroom at the Potsdam District No. 17 School. By 1872, the town of Potsdam had 36 district or common schools and employed 38 teachers. In 1954, Potsdam began the process of centralization, and within 10 years' time all the small community schools were closed.

FIFTH-GRADERS, 1921–1922. Teacher Mabel Cousins (far left) stands with her fifth-grade class at No. 8 Main Street. An unidentified student teacher sits in the back row.

Three

WORSHIP

THE GOSPEL CAR, C. 1900. During the 19th and early 20th centuries, itinerant missionaries and preachers delivered spiritual messages and provided religious services, particularly in rural areas. Potsdam was no exception in hosting its share of traveling evangelists. They preached in homes, from gospel wagons, in tents, and anywhere they could encourage folks to gather and listen to their message of salvation.

THE METHODIST CHURCH, MAIN STREET, THE 1880S. The first Methodist church in the village was built in 1821, on the corner of Main and Park Streets. It was known as the "white church." In 1860, a larger brick building (on left) was constructed on Main Street. The two-story parsonage (on right) was added to the Methodist property in 1882.

THE METHODIST CHURCH, 1903. The brick church was replaced with one constructed of Gouverneur marble, on the same site, in 1903. In 1967, the bell tower was deemed to be unsafe and was removed from the façade.

THE METHODIST SUNDAY SCHOOL CLASS, C. 1920. Members of the Sunday school class assemble for a picture.

TRINITY EPISCOPAL CHURCH, C. 1909. The boys' and men's choir prepare for an Easter service.

TRINITY EPISCOPAL CHURCH, 1885. Built in 1835, Trinity Church was modeled after Trinity Church in New York City, the home parish of the Clarkson family. The Clarksons donated half of Fall Island as well as building materials for the Federal-style church, which is constructed of Potsdam sandstone. The sandstone wall across the front of the property was added in 1870.

TRINITY EPISCOPAL CHURCH, 1900. By 1900, the congregation had grown in members, and the structure had undergone significant alterations, several funded by bequests of the Clarkson family. Of the original building, only the sidewalls, in the slab and binder masonry, remained. For new construction—including the façade and tower, chapel, and extended sanctuary—the new rough-ashlar method of construction was used. From 1893 to 1927, seven memorial stained-glass windows, created by the Tiffany Studios, were installed in the nave.

THE UNIVERSALIST CHURCH, c. 1900. This sandstone church, built in 1876 on Elm and Park Streets, replaced an earlier wooden structure. Services were held there until 1933, when the dwindling congregation voted to give the building to the village for use as a library. The structure was incorporated into the civic center in 1934, and later became the Potsdam Public Museum.

THE CATHOLIC APOSTOLIC CHURCH, C. 1910. Potsdam's Catholic Apostolic Church was organized in 1837, and was the first of its kind in the United States. The denomination began in Scotland about 1830; members were often called "Irvingites" because they followed the teachings of Englishman Edward Irving. This wooden church, at the corner of Maple and Pine Streets, was built in 1843 and enlarged in 1874. The church was legally dissolved in 1894, and the building was razed about 1918.

THE FIRST PRESBYTERIAN CHURCH, C. 1880. Located on the corner of Elm Street and Lawrence Avenue, this sandstone church was built between 1868 and 1872 in the Gothic Revival style. The brick building that formerly housed the Presbyterian Church had been sold to the state for the Potsdam Normal School, with the congregation retaining ownership of the pews and other furnishings. The church purchased the site for the new building (shown) from George Bonney. The Rev. Horatio Bogue was pastor during the construction.

THE PRESBYTERIAN CHURCH CHOIR, 1863. Members of the choir are, from left to right, as follows: (sitting) W. L. Knowles, J. H. Chandler, D. Chandler, and C. W. Bonney; (standing) F. H. Wilcox, ? Henry, ? Best, Lottie Fling, ? Slosson, ? Whitimore, Jasper Barnum, ? Bonney, ? Perro, and Herb Barnum.

ST. MARY'S ROMAN CATHOLIC CHURCH, C. 1910. In 1832, Father Salmon of Waddington held the first Mass for Potsdam Roman Catholics in the home of a Mr. Burke on Pierrepont Avenue. By the mid-1840s, services were held in a former house purchased from David Clarkson by Father MacKey; the house was blessed and named St. Mary's. It was located on Lawrence Avenue. Because of the growth of the Catholic population, it was soon possible to build a new church. The house was sold and moved to Clinton Street. The new gray wooden structure, built on the location of the previous frame building, was dedicated in 1859. The congregation grew rapidly from about 600 members in 1859 to 1,600 members in 1892. By this time, the congregation had again outgrown its building, and so the current edifice of sandstone was constructed next to the old church. Following the dedication of the new church, the old building was torn down.

THE FIRST BAPTIST CHURCH, WITH THE GEORGE BULLES HACK, C. 1910. Members of what is now the First Baptist Church of Potsdam began organizing about 1824, for the purpose of establishing a church. The congregation had no regular meeting house until 1858, when a wooden church was completed on the corner of Leroy and Elm Streets. On January 20, 1970, the church was completely destroyed by fire. The current Meeting House, at 24 Leroy Street, was purchased by the Baptist congregation in 1972.

THE FIRST CHURCH OF CHRIST, SCIENTIST, 1950. This Christian Science Church was organized in 1891, with members holding services in various homes until 1901. From 1901 to 1946, the church was on the corner of Main Street and Pierrepont Avenue. In 1946, the present Elm Street building was purchased; the initial service was held on Thanksgiving Day.

Four

PEOPLE AND HOMES

RICHMOND WAGONER ON THE TELEPHONE POLE, 1905. Richmond Wagoner was a telephone switchboard operator, wire chief, and trouble man for the Independent Telephone Company in Potsdam. The company was located in the rear of the J. R. Weston Store on Market Street, and was the first phone company in Potsdam. The telephone pole was located behind Weston's Store.

THE THATCHER HOUSE, 100 MARKET STREET, C. 1885. Built in the Italianate style c. 1870, this red brick house with a sandstone foundation was designed by its owner, Dr. Hervey D. Thatcher, a druggist and inventor of one of the first glass milk bottles.

FUN WITH THE FAMILY DOG, C. 1900. J. Daniel Lewis shares a lighthearted moment with his son, Leland A. Lewis, and the family pet. The Lewis farm was on Route 3.

Dr. Hervey Dexter Thatcher, c. 1900. Dr. Thatcher was born in Newport, New Hampshire, in 1835, and graduated from the Eclectic Medical Institute of Cincinnati, Ohio, in 1859. He came to Potsdam as a young man and became known primarily as a druggist and inventor. Thatcher married the former O. Adelaide Barnhart; the couple had no children. From 1860 to 1895, he operated a drug store, H. D. Thatcher & Co., at 19 Market Street. His numerous inventions included a glass milk bottle, Sugar of Milk Baking Powder, orange butter coloring, a paper bottle cap, several board games, and a paper milk carton. Thatcher's milk bottle led to the founding of the Thatcher Manufacturing Company on Depot Street. The company was eventually sold to businessmen in Elmira, New York, where it became the world's largest producer of glass milk bottles. Thatcher took out over 20 patents, and received awards for his products at the 1893 World's Fair in Chicago. He also served as a trustee of Clarkson College. Despite his successes, Thatcher died in poverty in 1925.

THE CLUB AT 10 ELM STREET, 1885. Built in the Federal style c. 1822 by surveyor John Call, this was the first house in the village to be constructed of Potsdam sandstone. The rear portions were added in the 1880s when it became the Potsdam Town Club. The building is now the Elks Club.

THE HOME AT 88 MARKET STREET, C. 1908. Bertrand H. Snell and wife Sara (Merrick) Snell settled here at the corner of Market and Garden Streets with their first daughter in 1908. Though typical of homes of the era, this lovely Queen Anne is notable because of the many famous people who visited or stayed as Congressman Snell's houseguests. Visitors included Presidents Taft, Harding, and Hoover, Governors Miller and Whitman, and several members of Congress.

OUT FOR A STROLL, 1915. Ada Powers enjoys a walk with her two children, Allen (in carriage) and Lawrence. Ada's husband, Raymond "Doc" Powers, was head of Clarkson's Electrical Engineering Department for nearly 40 years. The family made their home at 20 Bay Street and later (1924) at 21 Chestnut Street.

LAURA FORD BROWNELL, MILLINER, C. 1900. In 1901, Mrs. Brownell sold hats in her shop at the corner of Elm and Market Streets.

SARA AND GEORGE W. SISSON SR., C. 1868. George Wing Sisson (1829–1913) was born in Glens Falls, New York. He came to Potsdam with his family in 1867, and purchased a part-interest in a sawmill. Sisson wed Sarah Hamilton (1834–1916) in 1854. They were married for 59 years, and had eight children and 21 grandchildren. Many residents remember the grand Thanksgiving dinners, anniversary and birthday parties, and other celebrations enjoyed by the Sisson family and their guests. They had a zest for life and took pleasure in celebrating family.

THE SISSON HOUSE, SISSON STREET, C. 1920. George W. Sisson Jr. moved to this house, known as Hillview Farm, in 1887. He enlarged the house and added the front porch and pillars in 1909. Family celebrations were held here for generations. In addition to being actively involved in the family's Racquette River Paper Company, Sisson is credited as a pioneer in raising Jersey cattle in this area. Hillview Farm and its 460 acres were sold in 1958.

A Family Gathering, 1893. George Wing Sisson Sr. and his wife, Sarah Hamilton Sisson, are pictured here at the family home, Hillview Farm, on Sisson Road, just outside the village. The Sissons were married in 1854, and raised eight children. Sisson was one of the founders of the Racquette River Paper Company. Four generations of Sissons were active in the company and in the lumber business, as well as in fraternal organizations, church, and higher education. The Sisson family celebrations, especially Thanksgiving, were very festive. After the senior Sissons moved to 14 Leroy Street in 1903, family gatherings were still held at Hillview Farm, the home of George W. Sisson Jr.

THE WATKINS HOUSE, 14 LEROY STREET, C. 1880. Built in the Italianate style c. 1865 by Henry Watkins, this house was eventually purchased and remodeled by George Wing Sisson Sr.

THE SISSON HOUSE, 14 LEROY STREET, C. 1915. After purchasing the house from Henry Watkins in 1903, George Wing Sisson Sr. remodeled the home in the Classical mode, with a triangular pediment, portico, and columns, a favorite Sisson trademark. The house eventually became a fraternity.

NOBLE STRONG ELDERKIN, c. 1860. One of Potsdam's leading citizens, Elderkin (1810–1875) was a businessman, sheriff, and a member of the state militia, where he rose to the rank of brigadier general. He served as speaker of the New York State Assembly, and was a member of the board of trustees of the St. Lawrence Academy and later of the Potsdam Normal School.

THE LADIES VOLUNTEER AID ASSOCIATION, 1861. The wives and mothers of local soldiers wasted no time answering the call for linens, food, and warm clothing during the Civil War. In 1862, the organization was renamed the Ladies Auxiliary Relief Association, part of the Sanitary Commission of the United States (which became the American Red Cross). Among the ladies in the photograph are Mrs. Henry Knowles, Mrs. C. W. Leete, and Mrs. H. N. Redway.

GEN. EDWIN A. MERRITT, C. 1880. By the age of 17, Edwin A. Merritt, the great-grandson of a Lexington minuteman, had moved from Vermont to St. Lawrence County, where he farmed and taught school. At the St. Lawrence Academy, Merritt learned surveying. When a railroad was built connecting Watertown and Massena, he was in charge of laying track from Norwood to Canton. Merritt entered politics in 1859–1860 as a member of the state assembly. The Civil War led to his appointment as quartermaster of the 60th Regiment New York Volunteers. Under Governor Fenton, Merritt was appointed quartermaster general, where his duties included caring for the sick and disabled soldiers. His postwar career included serving as collector of the Port of New York and as consul general to London (England). General Merritt's interest in education led to Potsdam becoming the site of one of four state normal schools. He also served on the boards of Clarkson and St. Lawrence Universities. Merritt died in December 1916.

THE DAVID CLARKSON HOUSE, 30 LEROY STREET, C. 1885. One of the most elegant of the early slab-and-binder sandstone houses, this was the center of the Clarkson farm that stretched from Market Street to Elm Street and north to the village border. Built c. 1836, the house was purchased c. 1860 by Gen. Edwin A. Merritt and remained in the Merritt family until 1937. In more recent years, the house has been made into apartments.

DR. THOMAS B. STOWELL, PRINCIPAL OF POTSDAM NORMAL SCHOOL, C. 1905. A well-known scientist and teacher of the natural sciences, Dr. Stowell was considered Potsdam Normal School's first "progressive" administrator. As principal (1889–1909), he realized the importance of preparing highly qualified teachers. To that end, he encouraged experimentation, active research, and creative approaches to education.

THE BAYSIDE CEMETERY LODGE. Constructed of Potsdam sandstone in 1901, this unusual building was the cemetery sexton's residence for many years. Sandstone for the building and gateway was donated from the Clarkson quarry; skilled masons and stonecutters also contributed their labor free of charge.

THE JONATHAN WALLACE HOUSE, 99 MARKET STREET, C. 1890. This house was built by Jonathan Wallace using the slab-and-binder method of sandstone construction. The house was purchased in 1880 by James Lemon, harness maker. He added the front porch and ornamental gallery around the roof. In the 1860s, the south lawn had an elaborate rose garden and fountains, with many roses imported from England.

THE POTSDAM POLICE FORCE, 1915. In 1895, Samuel Maxfield, a Civil War veteran, was appointed the first police officer in Potsdam. As he made his nightly rounds (there was no day patrolman at the time), he was often accompanied by his mastiff, Major. In the next few years, day patrolman Eugene Smith was added to the force, followed by James Leahy. In 1903, Leahy became Potsdam's first chief of police, holding that position for many years. The officers pictured here also held town and county offices. Chief Leahy and Officer Smith were also deputy sheriffs; Officers Williams and Huntingdon were constables of the town of Potsdam. From left to right are the following: (first row) Chief Leahy and Officer Stone; (second row) Officers Smith, Williams, and Huntingdon.

THE LADIES ORCHESTRA, C. 1881. The First Grand Concert given by the Ladies Orchestra was held at the town hall in Potsdam, on November 4, 1881. Highlights included vocal solos by Jessie Crane, Allie Swift, and Nellie Brush; a horn solo by Nellie Brush; a violin duet by Gracie Howe and C. H. Pierce; and a cornet solo by C. H. Pierce.

THE POTSDAM MILITARY BAND, 1899. Potsdam bands may have evolved from the town band that went to the Civil War. In the 1880s and 1890s they marched in parades and gave street-corner concerts. Concerts at the "bird's nest," a platform in the large trees at the foot of Elm Street, required performers to enter across a board from an office building and play sitting down. The platform was eventually put on wheels and brought to concerts.

AMERICA'S FIRST TRAINED NURSE, 1873. Linda Richards (1841–1930) was born Melinda Ann Judson Richards, the daughter of an itinerant preacher. The family moved from Potsdam to Wisconsin and eventually to Vermont when Linda was very young. In 1873, she received her diploma from the New England Hospital for Women and Children in Roxbury, Massachusetts, becoming the first graduate of an American training school. Working in England with Florence Nightingale, establishing the first nursing school in Japan, and introducing home care for the poor in slum areas of Philadelphia are among Richards's many accomplishments. Her diploma is in the archives of the Smithsonian Institution.

POTSDAM'S FIRST TWO-STORY HOUSE, C. 1900. Liberty Knowles (1784–1859), Potsdam's first lawyer, built this house on Market Street in 1811. He spent his lifetime working to advance education and improve town infrastructure. In the 1920s, the house was owned by Hallen Ives. It was razed in 1938 to make way for the Kaplan Business Block.

GEORGE BULLES SR., C. 1920. George Bulles (born Boulet in Quebec) settled in Potsdam because of its size and active French community. By 1885, he was driving a hack, meeting trains and carrying shoppers to and from the business district. He purchased this Ford touring car in 1918. Decreased business and declining health forced Bulles to give up his stand at the corner of Market and Elm Streets in about 1928.

LAVINIA (1842–1926) AND THOMAS S. CLARKSON (1837–1894), C. 1860. Lavinia and Thomas S. Clarkson were two of the six children of Thomas Clarkson (1799–1873) and Elizabeth Clarkson (1810–1883). The family moved to Potsdam about 1840, and lived in the Homestead on Clarkson Hill. The Clarkson family had accumulated wealth in stocks and property in New York City. In spite of this advantage, all the Clarkson men learned a trade. Thomas S. and his brother Levinus ran the Clarkson farm, which consisted of more than 1,000 acres, until the death of Levinus in 1876. Thomas S. then encouraged and financed a variety of local businesses, including the Clarkson sandstone quarry. Lavinia, one of four Clarkson sisters, was known as the "quiet, reclusive" one. Little information is available about her life. Following the death of Thomas S. in 1894, his sisters established the Thomas S. Clarkson Memorial School of Technology, now Clarkson University, in his memory.

LAWN TENNIS, C. 1890. Members of the Clarkson family and friends enjoy a game of lawn tennis on the Clarkson Estate. In the background is the Homestead, home of Thomas (1799–1873) and Elizabeth Clarkson (1810–1883) and their children Ann Mary, Elizabeth, Frederica, Lavinia, Levinus, and Thomas S. (for whom the university is named). Annie Clarkson (1858–1929) is believed to be one of the tennis players.

ELIZABETH AND FREDERICA CLARKSON, 1908. Elizabeth Clarkson (1833–1918), on left, and Frederica Clarkson (1846–1909), on right, visit with ? Sherman, wife of the rector of Trinity Episcopal Church. The Clarkson sisters were generous donors to Trinity Church.

HOLCROFT, C. 1865. The original Clarkson mansion, Holcroft, was built c. 1822 by John C. Clarkson, the first family member to come to Potsdam. The mansard roof was added in 1853. The house is located on what is now known as the hill campus of Clarkson University.

THE CLARKSON CONSERVATORY AND GREENHOUSE, C. 1895. This completely furnished conservatory with functioning greenhouse was part of the property known as the Homestead, which included a large house and a barn. Thomas Clarkson and his wife, Elizabeth, came to live at the Homestead c. 1840. Their children, including Thomas S. (for whom the university is named), continued to reside there during their adulthood.

EMILIE CLARKSON MOORE, C. 1936. Born Emilie Valette Clarkson in 1863, she was the daughter of T. Streatfield and Ann Mary Clarkson, and the niece of Thomas S. Clarkson, for whom Clarkson University is named. Emilie married William Moore, and she was considered to be a talented artist and photographer. Emilie Clarkson Moore made generous donations to Clarkson College, Potsdam Hospital, and Trinity Church. She died in 1946.

THE REVEREND AND MRS. SHERMAN, C. 1908. The Reverend and Mrs. Sherman stand amid the great variety of plants in the Homestead conservatory on the Clarkson Estate. The Reverend Sherman was rector of Trinity Episcopal Church from 1905 to 1911. He and his wife resided at the Episcopal rectory on Main Street. They were often guests of Frederica, Elizabeth, and Lavinia Clarkson.

JULIA ETTIE CRANE, 1917. Considered a pioneer in music education, Julia Crane (1855–1923) was born near Potsdam. Her father was a farmer and businessman. An 1874 graduate of Potsdam Normal School, she taught in Potsdam's District School No. 8 until 1877. Her vocal studies took her to Boston, New York, and London. In 1884, after a number of years of giving private lessons, Crane joined Potsdam Normal's faculty, while still continuing her own music studies. With a deep interest in teaching methods, she became the director of the Normal Conservatory of Music. She organized the Crane Normal Institute of Music in 1886, the first school in the United States connected with a teacher training institution to train public school music teachers. Crane had many publications to her credit, and she was a founding member of Potsdam's Christian Science Church.

Dr. Helen M. Hosmer, c. 1955. Helen M. Hosmer (1898–1989) moved to Potsdam from Albany at the age of eight. In 1918, she graduated from the Potsdam Normal School and the Crane Institute as a voice major. She was offered a teaching position in 1922 by Julia Crane, and in 1930, she became director of the Crane School of Music. Dr. Hosmer held that position until her retirement in 1966. Appointed professor and dean emeritus of music at Potsdam College in 1967, she received international recognition as a conductor and choral adjudicator. Hosmer started the Crane Chorus in the early 1930s, involving guest conductors such as Nadia Boulanger and Robert Shaw. Hosmer earned degrees from Columbia University and honorary doctorates from St. Lawrence University and Clarkson College. Hosmer Hall on the Potsdam College campus was completed in 1974 and was named after this dedicated musician and teacher.

Five
EVERYDAY LIFE

MARKET STREET, THE 1920S. Parallel and angled parking facilitated the movement of traffic on Market Street in the 1920s. The corner of Elm and Market Streets is to the left. The Racquette River can be seen at the far end of the street.

A WATER MAIN INSTALLATION, C. 1870. Workmen take a break while installing a water main in front of the Liberty Knowles house on the east side of Market Street, across from the head of Depot Street. Note the pieces of sandstone sidewalk piled around the site.

WEST MARKET STREET, C. 1866. This is an early view of downtown Potsdam's business district. The three-story brick building with arched windows and doorways, at center of photograph, was H. D. Thatcher & Company's Drug and Chemical Business. The one-story Frontier Bank (1853–1866), two buildings to the left, is recognizable by its pillar façade. Notice the hitching posts and elegantly wide sandstone sidewalks.

STREET REPAIR, C. 1915. Men from Christy and Clough work on installing cement curbing in Potsdam. The company's nameplates can still be found on some village sidewalks.

THE ROAD CREW, C. 1915. Workers stand alongside their steamroller at the corner of Elm and Market Streets.

REBUILDING THE STONE DAM, C. 1902. These men were part of the work force that rebuilt the stone dam across the Racquette River at Fall Island. Batchelder & Sons furniture factory is to the right; the Clarkson Land Office is the sandstone building in the middle of the photograph.

CANAL STREET, 1910. Workmen continue on a project to cover the canal on Canal Street.

THE WATERWORKS, C. 1900. Shortly after the May 5, 1871 flood, this sandstone building and distribution system were constructed on Raymond Street. A tannery business had previously occupied the space. A bond issue, to be paid off by 1913, financed the waterworks' original cost of $40,000. Untreated water was pumped from the Racquette River using the Holly system, through nearly 12 miles of piping.

SANDSTONE BUILDING CONSTRUCTION, C. 1917. Musicians take advantage of a work break at a construction site on the grounds of the original Potsdam Normal School.

SPECIAL DELIVERY C. 1910. Mark Salls stands beside his Potsdam rural U.S. mail wagon.

THE ARLINGTON HOTEL STATION WAGON, C. 1913. Walter A. Tidd of Harrisville began a five-year lease of the Arlington Hotel starting in 1913. This driver and his pair of horses picked up passengers from the train depot for their hotel stay. One of the first-floor businesses visible in this photograph is the New Arlington Bakery at 6 Market Street, run by Edgar F. Covey.

NO SIGN OF SPRING, MARCH 1900. This scene in front of Goldsmith's One Price Clothing House, at 14 Market Street, shows that there was still a lot of snow accumulation in early March. Note the clothing displayed outside the stores.

THE CORNER OF MARKET AND MAPLE STREETS, C. 1920. This winter scene shows the bridge leading to Fall Island, with Trinity Church to the left. The sandstone building on the right was constructed in 1840, and was originally used as a leather shop and tannery.

THE NEW FLEET OF SNOWPLOWS. Town of Potsdam superintendent Edward E. Wright did much to update equipment, including the addition of these trucks during his tenure from 1928 to 1933. Previously, a snowplow was attached to a truck owned by Herb Fearl, a Potsdam oil dealer. That truck covered all the roads in the entire town. This photograph was taken at the town barn on Madrid Avenue.

THE ICY AFTERMATH, DECEMBER 18, 1942. Thick ice clings to B. O. Kinney's Drug Store at 19 Market Street the day after a fire caused over $300,000 in damage to the building. Local firefighters and five assisting fire departments fought the blaze for over 12 hours in temperatures that were well below zero. Three stores were destroyed; no one was injured. James E. Doyle Jr. was the fire chief at the time.

THE FIREMEN'S HALL, C. 1900. Potsdam firemen stand in front of the firemen's hall, formerly the Methodist church, on the corner of Park and Main Streets. To the left is an important item of early firefighting equipment, the hand-drawn hose cart. At the far right is Frank Cassada, fire chief. In 1913, the cornerstone for the new brick fire station was laid at this site.

THE FIRE AT THE INTERSECTION OF WATER AND MARKET STREETS, C. 1910. Potsdam's steam fire engine is at work here on Water Street. The buildings in the background are, from left to right, Tucker's Grocery; Tom's Barbershop, which included a pool and billiards room; the Riverside Hotel; and a vacant structure.

THE POTSDAM FIRE DEPARTMENT, C. 1930. Public approval for a new fire station was gained on July 16, 1912. The decision was made to place it at the corner of Main and Park Streets, where the original wooden firemen's hall had existed since 1860. The cornerstone for the new station was laid on July 17, 1913, following a parade up Main Street headed by the Potsdam Band. The photograph shows volunteer firefighters c. 1930 and their equipment, which included a steam fire engine and horse-drawn hose and chemical wagon; the first motor truck, a Brockway Hose and Chemical Truck, rebuilt in 1925 as a ladder-hose and chemical combination; an American La France 750 GMP Pumper; a Sanford 500-gallon-per-minute pumper; and a Packard touring car donated by Mrs. W. A. Moore and rebuilt into a squad truck.

THE STAR THEATER. Built in 1913, this theater's façade featured hand-painted murals by artist Irving E. Shanafelt. The Ives brothers owned the Star, which seated nearly 500. Louise Cook accompanied the movie shows on the piano. During the theater's opening week in 1913, admission topped 4,000. True to the *Courier-Freeman* news article of that week, the Star played "high class photo motion plays" which pleased "large audiences daily."

THE RIALTO THEATER, 1924. This movie theater at 22–24 Market Street offered "the best and latest pictures." Opened in the early 1920s, the Rialto had closed by 1960. Note the large poster in the window advertising *The Enchanted Cottage*, a silent film starring Richard Barthelmess.

A HOLIDAY TREAT, DECEMBER 22, 1949. For many years, the Potsdam Police Department sponsored a free movie and treats for local children at the Rialto Theater on Market Street. The policeman is Harry Wheeler.

POLICEMEN AT WORK, 1947. Acting Chief of Police Harry Wheeler (left) is shown here with Ed Fuhr.

THE FRONTIER HOUSE AND LIVERY, C. 1900. This small hotel or boardinghouse was located at 31 Depot Street. Fred LaDuke established it in 1886, with his wife serving as "culinary supervisor." Rent was a modest $1 per day. In later years, the hotel was run by David Dishaw (c. 1901) and William Barclay (c. 1913). Its location made the Frontier House a favorite of railroad personnel. A livery for the stabling of customers' horses was attached to the building. The business closed in the early 1920s.

THE ICE STORM, MARCH 27, 1913. This ice storm lasted for 36 hours, with Potsdam among the hardest-hit communities. The combination of ice and wind was so damaging to elm trees that a corps of forestry experts was brought in from Rochester to prune and trim the trees. Unusual flooding was reported on the Racquette River, with water running over the retaining wall on Raymond Street.

THE AMERICAN EXPRESS COMPANY, C. 1900. The American Express Company's delivery sled makes a gradual turn in front of the Citizen's Bank at the corner of Elm and Market Streets. Luna S. Howard, holding the reins, worked for the company as a driver and clerk from the early 1900s into the 1940s.

WINTER TRAVEL C. 1920. Dr. Hugh A. Grant takes his cutter out along Market Street with an unidentified companion. He and wife Margaret and their two sons lived at 47 Elm Street. Dr. Grant studied at McGill University and throughout Europe before joining the practice of Dr. James McKay, and later opening his own office.

THE POTSDAM DEPOT, C. 1900. The first depot, constructed of wood, opened in 1854 and served travelers until 1914. Originally, the railroad had bypassed Potsdam. Beginning in 1852, Potsdam men formed the Potsdam Railroad Company and built tracks to join the Northern line at Potsdam Junction (Norwood). The Frontier House, where travelers could rent rooms, is at the right.

THE NEW POTSDAM DEPOT, C. 1925. On June 1, 1914, the New York Central's new sandstone station was dedicated. It was located to the right of the old depot, 20 yards closer to the river. By 1960, New York Central had stopped all passenger service north of Syracuse. In 1980, the depot was moved several hundred feet to make way for construction of the Potsdam Relief Route (the Bypass). The depot now houses a restaurant.

RIVER RECREATION, 1900. Hattie Smith (front) and friends enjoy canoeing on the Racquette River. John Frederick offered canoe rentals by the hour at 20 Bay Street. Today, the Racquette River continues to be appreciated by boating enthusiasts.

WADING IN THE RACQUETTE RIVER, C. 1910. Cousins Marion Sisson Weed and Helen Safford Reynolds, granddaughters of George Wing Sisson Sr., wade in the Racquette River at Hewittville.

THE WEST SIDE OF MARKET STREET, C. 1910. The changing times are evident in the various modes of transportation shown on downtown Market Street.

THE EAST SIDE OF MARKET STREET, C. 1910. The use of awnings kept sidewalks and storefronts cool.

DRIVING WITH FRIENDS, 1910. Arthur Wescott is at the wheel of this 1908 white Buick parked outside the Potsdam Auto Garage, at 2 Willow Street. David Gregg, the garage proprietor, is standing in the doorway in the white coat.

AN INDIAN MOTORCYCLE WITH SIDECAR, 63 MARKET STREET, C. 1920. A gentleman and his lady companion pose for this photograph at the corner of Market and Willow Streets.

EARL CLARK'S RIG, C. 1910. Earl Clark, proprietor of Meadow Brook Dairy Farm, and deliverer of Aerated Milk and Sweet Cream, takes a break from work to give neighborhood children a ride in his donkey cart.

EDWARD LA DUKE AND PARTNER, C. 1910. Edward La Duke's daughter holds on to dad's horse while he makes a delivery for the Carrier Spring Water Company.

THE WEST BRIDGE, C. 1880. In 1877, the wooden East and West Bridges were replaced with iron bridges. The total cost of the new construction was $7,902. The bridges lasted until 1922, when concrete bridges were erected. This view shows the (iron) West Bridge, crossing the Racquette River, leading to Fall Island. Trinity Episcopal Church is to the right.

THE EAST BRIDGE, 1924. The concrete East and West Bridges were constructed in 1922 to replace the iron bridges. This Clarence Premo photograph shows a view of downtown Potsdam, looking east on Maple Street. On the left side of Main Street were the Arlington Inn, Potsdam Feed and Coal office, and the Great Atlantic & Pacific Tea Company. William E. Murphy's bakery featured Butter-Nut-Bread, proclaimed to be "Sweet as Butter; Rich as a Nut."

THE ALBION BARBERSHOP, C. 1900. This barbershop was located in the Albion Hotel on Elm Street. Note the racks of shaving mugs along the back wall. The barber in the center is Maurice Osgood.

A FUNERAL PROCESSION, 1924. This procession, led by a group of fraternal or religious associates of the deceased, passed Trinity Episcopal Church, Maple Street, on its way to St. Mary's Roman Catholic Church on Lawrence Avenue.

THE RACQUETTE RIVER PAPER COMPANY FIRE DEPARTMENT, JUNE 1925. Firemen assemble in front of the Racquette River Paper Company. George W. Sisson Jr., president of the company, is second from the right; Chief Robert Mulligan is third from the right.

CONSTRUCTION OF THE CIVIC CENTER, JULY 1934. The old town hall stood on this spot on Park Street from 1875 to 1933. In 1934, with funding from the Works Progress Administration, the town hall was razed, and a new civic center was constructed in its place. The new structure reused sandstone from the old building. The Universalist church (far left), given to the village by a dwindling congregation, became a part of the civic center as the new public library.

WINTER FUN, 1937. The Normal School's toboggan slide on Pierrepont Avenue was built by the Civilian Conservation Corps. The course was 542 feet in length, "emerging upon the river bed." The chute's metal lining was considered to be an experiment, designed to protect tobogganers from side wall (wood) slivers. The sliding surface itself was made from ice blocks sawed from the river.

THE POTSDAM GENERAL HOSPITAL, 1932. This 54-bed hospital on Leroy Street opened October 17, 1932, with eight patients who had been transferred from the "cottage" hospital a block away on Waverly Street. That facility had been established in 1925, through persistent efforts of the Village Nursing Association, headed by Adelaide Norris. Opening ceremonies for the new hospital drew a crowd of nearly 1,500. William Distin of Saranac Lake and Thomas Phillips of Watertown designed the building.

THE POTSDAM CORNET BAND, 1884. This group of local musicians provided music for parades and other special occasions. From left to right are the following: (first row) G. W. Sisson Jr., F. W. Moon, and E. Hall; (second row) B. E. Leete, W. Pert, C. Vance, W. Denmark, Herbert Dishaw, E. Wells, and H. Wagner; (third row) F. Rivers, H. Watkins, J. Wallace, ? Tromblay, J. B. Davies, F. Spaulding, J. Friecien, and E. Crane.

A BOATING EXCURSION, C. 1884. Two couples explore a quiet cove on the Racquette River.

Six

POTSDAM, THE NATION, AND THE WORLD

COMPANY A, 92ND REGIMENT, C. 1862. The 92nd Regiment was the second unit from Potsdam to enter the War Between the States. Jonah Sanford of Hopkinton was instrumental in obtaining authorization to organize and train a regiment in Potsdam. One thousand strong, the troops left Potsdam in 1862, and mustered out in 1865.

CAPT. THOMAS HICKEY OF THE 164TH REGIMENT, C. 1863. By 1862, it was clear that President Lincoln's call for 75,000 volunteers would be insufficient. In St. Lawrence County, James O'Connor and Thomas Hickey organized a company of soldiers to join Gen. Michael Corcoran's Irish Legion. The group became Company A of the 164th Regiment. A year later, Captain Hickey assumed command. Half of the company was from Potsdam; most, like Canadian-born Hickey, were born outside the United States. The soldiers' ages ranged from 17 to 44. Members of Company A included laborers, skilled craftsmen, and professionals. The majority were farmers. The company took part in some of the war's heaviest fighting, including the Battle of Cold Harbor on June 3, 1864, in which Hickey was mortally wounded. This photograph shows Hickey (seated, fifth from the left) with the officers of Company A.

Col. Samuel Marsh, c. 1861. Samuel Marsh, a Potsdam physician, teacher, and lay preacher, received military instruction at Norwich University. Col. Samuel Marsh, fatally wounded at the Battle of Gaines' Mill, Virginia, in 1862, was the first Potsdam resident to die in the Civil War. Marsh Post, Grand Army of the Republic, No. 214, was named in his honor.

Lt. John Vance, c. 1862. Lt. John Vance helped organize Company F of the 16th Regiment. He served as a member of the signal corps until 1863. After returning to Potsdam, Vance practiced law and was elected surrogate judge of St. Lawrence County. He died in 1899.

THE CIVIL WAR VETERANS REUNION, C. 1900. This photograph shows members of Marsh Post No. 214, Grand Army of the Republic. The post was chartered in 1881 and was organized with 45 members a year later. Their headquarters on Raymond Street was eventually moved to Market Street. The group disbanded in 1931.

THE DRAFT, 1918. One of the last groups of World War I draft registrants poses in front of Local Draft Board, Division No. 2, St. Lawrence County, located at 23 Market Street. The group was part of the draft list issued on September 12, 1918; physicals were postponed because of the worldwide Spanish influenza epidemic. The men were inducted into the army and navy on November 4, 1918, one week before the armistice was achieved.

WORLD WAR I, THE HOME FRONT, C. 1917. Potsdam residents supported the war effort in many ways. Parades raised money for the Potsdam war chest, which would be used to provide materials for Red Cross workers and "all legitimate causes arising out of the war." Bonds were purchased from the United States government under the Liberty Loan Program.

WORLD WAR I ENDS, NOVEMBER 11, 1918. Sirens and bells rang out at 4 a.m. on November 11, 1918. Church services began at 10:30 a.m. By 2 p.m. the largest parade ever seen had assembled. The Potsdam Band was preceded by police Chief James Leahy, attorney Frank Cubley (Uncle Sam), parade marshal Frank Baum and M. V. B. Ives's large flag. Businesses were closed. Speeches, music, dancing in the streets, and a huge bonfire lasted through the night. Joy was unconfined.

CALVIN COOLIDGE AND BERTRAND SNELL, 1926. Bert Snell (right) was educated at Potsdam Normal School and Amherst College. Among his close friends at Amherst was Calvin Coolidge (left), future governor of Massachusetts. Snell was elected to the House of Representatives in 1915, and served as chairman of the powerful Rules Committee from 1919 to 1931. When President Harding died in 1923, Vice President Coolidge assumed the office. Coolidge was elected president in his own right a year later.

A FUTURE PRESIDENT VISITS POTSDAM, 1929. New York's Democratic governor Franklin Delano Roosevelt traveled north on July 24, 1929, and met with Republican congressman Bert Snell in front of the State Normal School building in Potsdam. Four years later, Roosevelt would occupy the White House. Snell would serve as minority leader in the House of Representatives from 1931 to 1938. In 1937, the two clashed over Roosevelt's plan to reorganize the Supreme Court.

WAR GAMES, 1940. In July and August 1940, some 15 months before Pearl Harbor, St. Lawrence County hosted between 75,000 and 100,000 soldiers, plus more than 100 aircraft, in the largest peacetime military maneuvers in the history of North America. A "Blue" army moving out of Plattsburgh by way of Potsdam failed to seize Watertown from the defending "Black" army. The event gave the United States a realistic test of its military capability under harsh conditions.

THE 101ST MASSACHUSETTS REGIMENT, 1940. This regiment participated in the war games of August 1940. Despite the seriousness of the event, regimental bands performed locally and a 300-piece U.S. Army band gave a concert in front of the Potsdam Civic Center.

AMERICA'S FIRST PEACETIME DRAFT, JANUARY 1941. Relations between the United States and the Axis nations were so strained by early 1941 that the United States instituted its first peacetime draft. Here, the first group to leave Potsdam is photographed with several members of the draft board in January 1941.

THE ARMISTICE DAY PARADE, NOVEMBER 11, 1946. Despite the rain, nearly 600 people took part in the 1946 Armistice Day Parade in Potsdam, while large numbers of people filled the business district to watch. Planned by the Roy D. Graves Post Veterans of Foreign Wars and Frank Barclay Post American Legion, the procession featured Potsdam veterans as well as representatives from other towns.

Seven
SPECIAL DAYS

GOING GREYHOUND, 1946. Crane Music students, many sporting bobby sox and saddle shoes, board a bus in front of the Presbyterian Church, corner of Elm Street and Lawrence Avenue, in March 1946. Accompanied by Marie Schuette, head of the Department of Music Practice Teaching, the group was traveling to attend the Music Educator's National Conference in Cleveland.

THE CIRCUS TRAIN WRECK, 1889. On August 22, 1889, the Barnum & Bailey Circus, en route to Montreal, Quebec, from Gouverneur, New York, traveled in three trains, running minutes apart.

THE CIRCUS TRAIN WRECK, 1889. An axle broke on the second train, causing six cars to pile into each other near Clark's Crossing on the Potsdam-Norwood Road. The train was carrying elephants, horses, and camels.

THE CIRCUS TRAIN WRECK, 1889. No human lives were lost, but 28 horses, 2 camels, and a mule were killed in the wreck.

THE CIRCUS TRAIN WRECK, 1889. In spite of the devastation caused by the wreck, the local residents took full advantage of the curious diversion offered by the sight of the rare animals and their exotic keepers (shown).

COLLEGIATE ICE SCULPTURE, CLARKSON, 1943. This patriotic ice sculpture was part of the Normal-Clarkson Annual Winter Carnival, first held in 1931. The carnival was the idea of Murray Walker, director of the Clarkson Hockey Association, and Eunice Badger of Potsdam State's athletic department.

COLLEGIATE ICE SCULPTURE, POTSDAM STATE, 1943. Ice sculptures were included in the Winter Carnival, which was created to encourage cooperative festivity between the two colleges, and included activities such as a parade, hockey games, speed skating, and a dance. In more recent years, snowy pursuits like those pictured here have been discontinued due to unpredictable weather.

A FUNERAL PROCESSION, C. 1890. The horse-drawn hearse is accompanied by members of a fraternal order as they proceed down Elm Street.

A CIRCUS PARADE, MAY 5, 1894. Madrid native George Cole partnered with Potsdam businessman Allan Lockwood to create a circus with a definite Potsdam flavor. Preparations for the parade were completed at the John May farm and employed the efforts of local blacksmiths, wheelwrights, tailors, milliners, dressmakers, and painters. Crowds enthusiastically greeted the parade on Market Street, where small boys ran beside Modoc, the four-ton "outlaw" elephant.

THE GLORIOUS FOURTH, 1901. Crowds lined Market Street at 8:00 a.m. sharp for the start of a "monster patriotic demonstration." Celebrations began with the "grand serenade of bands" followed by a "parade of terribles." Prizes of $8 for most artistic and most terrible costumes were awarded. The Knights of the Macabees made an impressive showing in their new uniforms. Sporting events and fireworks were part of the celebration.

THE CANOE RACES, 1901. During the July 4th celebration in 1901, spectators watched the canoe races from the East Bridge. The iron bridge was built in 1850, and stood until about 1920. Fall Island and Trinity Church are in the background.

THE BASEBALL SCOREBOARD, OCTOBER 8, 1927. Fans gathered in front of the St. Lawrence County utilities building at 38 Market Street to follow the progress of game four of the 1927 World Series between the New York Yankees and Pittsburgh Pirates. Men standing on a platform wrote in an account of the game's action, which they received by radio. The top left of the scoreboard reveals the Yankee lineup that defeated the Pirates in four straight games: Combs, center field; Koenig, shortstop; Ruth, right field; Gehrig, first base; Meusel, left field; Lazzeri, second base; Dugan, third base; Collins, catcher; Durt, pinch hitter; and Moore, pitcher.

THE FIREMEN'S ANNUAL REVIEW, 1927. The Potsdam Fire Department held an annual review to demonstrate the capabilities of its equipment. The first motor truck, a hose and chemical combination, had been purchased by the village in 1918. The Racquette River provided an unlimited source of water. To the right, parallel to the river, is Water Street, which no longer exists. That area is now the site of the Clarkson Inn.

BETTER THAN GOLD, NOVEMBER 20, 1916. Sarah (Benson) and Martin V. B. Ives greeted more than 200 family members and friends beneath a bell of chrysanthemums in their Pierrepont Avenue home in November 1916. The couple's 50th-anniversary party included recitations, poems by Mrs. E. J. Austin, and music by Julia Crane. The GAR and WRC marched from their hall to the Ives's home, accompanied by fife and drum. Refreshments were served by a "bevy of charming young ladies." The guests bid their farewells after singing, "Blest be the Tie That Binds." Martin V. B. Ives and his brother Hallan were successful businessmen. The land that became Ives Park was given to the village by Hallan in his brother's name.

OFF TO THE RACES, C. 1900. The racehorse in this scene represents one of the popular activities held at the Potsdam Fairground. The grandstand is visible in the background. The Racket Valley and St. Regis Valley Agricultural and Horticultural Society organized the first Potsdam Fair in 1870. It was a yearly event through 1927. The former fairground property is now occupied by Potsdam's public schools.

PICTURES WHILE YOU WAIT, C. 1910. Jacob F. Clow (left) was ready to snap your photograph at the Potsdam Fairground. He and son Jacob Jr. ran the Superior Art Studio, which also made picture frames. The business was located at Clow's residence, 1½ Willow Street, from c. 1893 to 1933.

THE PAINTING BEE, C. 1914. Potsdam citizens gather together to paint the Floral Hall for the Potsdam Fair. Known as the Racket Valley and St. Regis Valley Fair when it was established in 1870, the fair featured horse racing, side shows, and domestic and garden produce competitions, as well as a variety of rides.

EASTER BONNETS, C. 1910. The Duffy-Rivers Dry Goods Company occupied the Cox Building at 5–7 Market Street for 25 years. In the 1940s, this location housed McCarthy's Clothing Store; Lewis and Co. took over the premises from the late 1940s until 1972. It is currently Maxfield's Restaurant.

THE WEDDING DAY, REV. AND MRS. ALFRED ERNEST PAGE, 1891. Alfred Ernest Page was born in Potsdam in 1866, and was educated at the Potsdam Normal School and Drew Theological Seminary. Page served as minister to churches in Colton, Parishville, and several other small towns. He married Celia Robinson of Colton in 1891. The couple had one daughter.

THE WEDDING CELEBRATION, APRIL 21, 1908. This photograph shows the interior of the studios of Harriet Crane Bryant and Julia E. Crane at the Crane Institute of Music on Main Street. The rooms were decorated for the wedding of Barbara Crane Moore and John T. Lloyd. The bride was the daughter of Harriet and Julia's sister, Jessie Crane Moore.

THE WEDDING DAY, MRS. A. RAYMOND POWERS, C. 1908. Alfred Raymond Powers and his bride, Ada W., were married c. 1908. Professor Powers, known as "Doc," began teaching at Clarkson College in 1909, and was a full-time faculty member in the electrical engineering department until 1956. The couple lived at 21 Chestnut Street.

THE WEDDING DAY, MRS. WILLIAM W. G. PECK, C. 1910. Mrs. William W. G. Peck (Gertrude S.) sits for a photograph on her wedding day. Her husband worked for the Northern Power Company, and by 1919 he was the manager of the Arlington Hotel. The couple lived at 59 Elm Street.

A NORMAL HALLOWEEN, C. 1920. These bewitching beauties presented a skit at the annual Potsdam Normal School Halloween Party. In 1927, a crowd of 600 attended this popular fall event. The party included a grand march, costume awards, and vaudeville entertainment in the auditorium. Pictured from left to right are Ruth Sisson Bynam, Alice Sterling, Emma Morgan Keeler, Marie R. O'Connor, Marion Pert White, Marjorie Sisson White, unidentified, and Margaret Stuart Reynolds.

SCHOOL DAYS, C. 1920. A group of young schoolchildren practice on a variety of musical instruments. Their classroom is decorated for the Christmas season.

THATCHER'S BUTTER COLOR AT THE WORLD'S FAIR, 1893. Mrs. Roberts demonstrates Dr. Hervey D. Thatcher's Butter Color at the 1893 Chicago World's Fair. Thatcher was a Potsdam inventor and druggist who had many patents to his credit. Farmers used his Butter Color during the winter, spring, and fall to give their butter a "June" appearance, which would bring them a higher price for their product. A 25¢ bottle could color about 500 pounds of butter. Nearly 27 million people attended the Chicago World's Fair, including many St. Lawrence County residents who took advantage of 10-day excursions offered by the Rome, Watertown, and Ogdensburg railroad.

THE CLASS DAY PROGRAM IN THE PARK, C. 1910. As part of Commencement Week festivities for the Potsdam Normal School graduation, students took part in the ivy procession. Led by their class president, the seniors marched out two-by-two, escorted by the juniors.

THE CLASS DAY PROGRAM, IVY CHAIN, C. 1910. Normal school students carried a chain of ivy and sang as they marched through the park. The procession was followed by speeches and more music.

CLARKSON COLLEGE, 1908. An academic procession, possibly a graduation, passes in front of Clarkson's Old Main building.

GRADUATION DAY, POTSDAM STATE TEACHERS COLLEGE, C. 1950. Graduates march across the lawn of the normal school building on Park Street. In 1942, the Potsdam Normal School became Potsdam State Teachers College, and shortly thereafter, the college began relocating to the Pierrepont Avenue campus. The college continued to use this building (now Snell Hall) until about 1958, when the move to the new campus was completed.

A LOGJAM, C. 1910. Ice floes and logs combine to damage the Sissonville bridge.

THE SQUIRREL HUNT BANQUET, C. 1925. A group of Potsdam businessmen attended the Squirrel Hunt Banquet at the Arlington Hotel. The hunters were divided into two teams, with the winners being treated to a banquet by the losers. Identified individuals seated on the left side of the table are, from front to back, as follows: (third from left) coach Ernest A. Blood of the Potsdam Normal School; (fifth from left) George Cook, jeweler; (seventh from left) Joseph Coleman, blacksmith; and (eighth from left) Nathan Clark, supervisor. Identified individuals seated on the right side of the table are, from front to back, as follows: (first from right) Willett Smith, car salesman; (second from right) William Bradish, merchant; (third from right) Walter Goodrich, plumber; (fourth from right) Fred Benson, merchant; (sixth from right) George Barnum; (seventh from right) Dan Blackmon, auto dealer; and (eighth from right) Frank Cassidy, mayor.

HERBERT HOOVER DEDICATING THE BOYS' CLUB, OCTOBER 7, 1945. Former President Herbert Hoover served as chairman of the board of directors of the Boys' Clubs of America. Formerly the Grange Hall, this building was a memorial to the young men from the area who had given their lives in the world wars. The building was sold in 1955, and is now Temple Beth-El. Standing in the front row on the stage are, from left to right, William F. Anderson; Bertrand Snell; President Hoover; George Sisson III; Fr. Joseph L. Tierney, pastor of St. Mary's Catholic Church; and Daniel Chase.

THE POTSDAM AIRPORT, 1947. This photograph was taken on the occasion of the first "breakfast flight" to Malone from Potsdam's Damon Field, on Sunday, August 3, 1947.

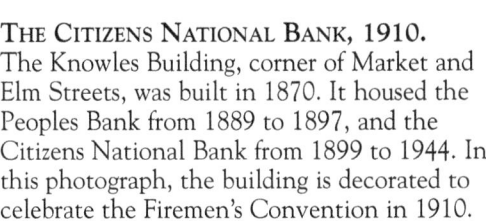

CRANE ABROAD, THE EXPERIMENTAL GROUP, 1936. Beginning in 1933 with 10 Crane Institute freshmen, Helen Hosmer (second row, second from the left) formed a group to explore the practicality of various educational innovations. A five-month trip to Europe was an essential element, including concentrated study in Berlin, Paris, and London. The group attended lectures, musical programs, and festivals, with emphasis on total immersion in the culture of each country.

THE CITIZENS NATIONAL BANK, 1910. The Knowles Building, corner of Market and Elm Streets, was built in 1870. It housed the Peoples Bank from 1889 to 1897, and the Citizens National Bank from 1899 to 1944. In this photograph, the building is decorated to celebrate the Firemen's Convention in 1910.

A RECORD LOAD OF LOGS, 1920. Ed La Vine of Potsdam drove this rig that carried "the largest load of pulp wood ever drawn out of the woods by a single team of horses." The 12-cord load of 4-foot logs was 10 feet wide, 10 feet high, and 18 feet long. The load was hauled 10 miles to the Racquette River, where it was floated down to the Racquette River Paper Company in the spring. Others shown in this photograph are George Hutchins, Amy Ames, Frank Bellinger, Jack Creighton, William Hammond, Frank Preston, and Elmer Watson.

www.ingramcontent.com/pod-product-compliance
Lightning Source LLC
Chambersburg PA
CBHW050541110426
42813CB00008B/2221